Poems I Wrote While Watching TV

ISBN 1-59971-340-3

Book & Cover design by Mario Dzurila

Some of these poems originally appeared in the following print and electronic publications: *Can We Have Our Ball Back?*, *3am Magazine*, *Prague Literary Review*, *Megaera*, *Minima*, *Versal*, *Pretend I Am Someone Else*, *Scarecrow*, *The Paris Beating Hearts Pit*, and *Stimulus*. Thanks to all those editors.

www.books.blatt.cz

Produced with quality and care by *PrintHouse* in Prague, Czech Republic, providing high quality publishing services at optimal prices.
www.etiskarna.cz

First Edition

Poems I Wrote While Watching TV

Words by Travis Jeppesen
Images by Jeremiah Palecek

BLATT BOOKS
PRAGUE — NEW YORK

1.

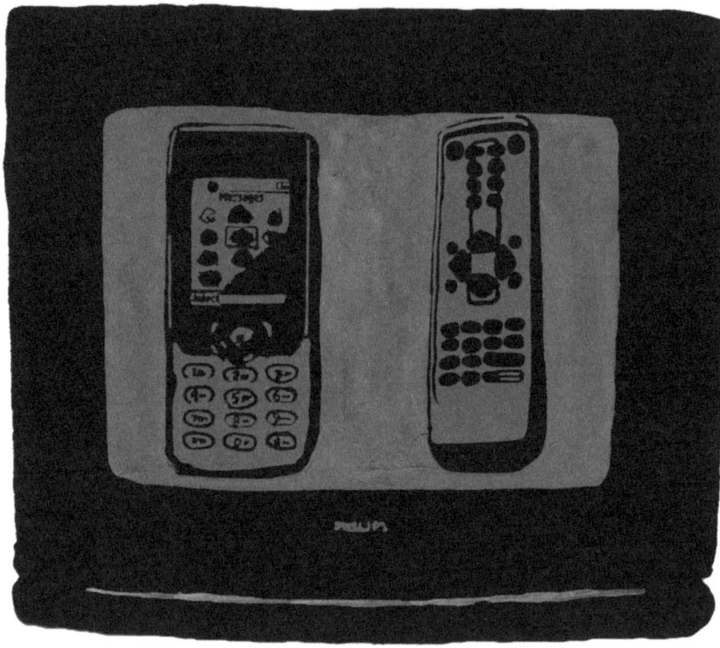

I see through every televised illusion
Word spacing corresponds to handwriting
Between the lines
Of some producer's coke binge

I hate actors
In real life you see through
So easily to their insecurities
It's like they don't know
To hide them.
Lithe and vulnerable as the
Bottle of wine they so timidly
Consume, like it's not theirs to
The touch. All of America looks
The same I realize from the
Distance of two years and
A foreign screen.

Nebulous Spectre

Pieces of matter transformed into holes.
Leave the pieces at salvation's doorstep.
A million different ways of coming apart now.
It seems like the forevers once knew my sandwich.
Not anymore. So much
Passion in those files, the poisson in our archive,
Our history of lightness.
Deepness dwells inside the running man.
So many different spheres of inactivity competing to combine
the two blank factors.
Sanitize backlaunch.
We haven't slept together yet.
My human warmth blues get me down style.
Splurge into forgiveness; the puppet trope's battle.

When the buttock soars...

Present escapes flashes of transplanted genus. Know how
Beneficial icy snatches of paradise can be when you're singing
the praises of the whale.
Dark splotches matter deeply.

Day finishes off its inevitable fade with
a whiff of indigestion, knocks off the
steamroller "highly unlikely," cough
crackles out on the sound waves, jerk
with happiness out of the rest, no having
vision. It's tough being there at
times.

Some children beat up Beethoven;
He writes a song about it.
Black-eyed beauty cries;
Steven Seagal isn't fast enough.

Velký Český Country Zpěvník

Osmosis on the scene of
someone else's palate. Kitchen

appliances dance past us; the butcher
knife stabs the hamburger through

the eye. There's no fireplace in the
kitchen so we light a match to imi-

tate the scent. A cook shows us how
they cook potatoes in another country;

trees gnaw through wind. Mustardman
wishing he could grasp the subtlety

of that cut, but lost fins of dayglow
offer only shimmer in the distant eye.

He speculates it's an art as he reaches
for his gun. It's a humorless drama

and the prisoners have already been
deposited in the nearest ocean, where

their skin can be heard to sizzle like
those eggs in the frying pan, as

they await some shark's jaws to
rescue them from pungent stains of

life's promise. Another marvelous weekend.

Paean to the Weatherwoman

She offers us a haze of images,
then explains what we're seeing.
If we step outside, we'll may-
be find the confirmation of her
computer-generated landscapes. Though
fake, it's another flavor to rub
on your armpit. The baby jumps
into a well of tiramisu... Fahrenheit,

Or Celsius? it asks the hollywood
sign, and every laundry detergent
becomes a pedophile's daydream. Then,
to switch the machine, yellow car
drives through sex, the gods bowl
over to worship a stain. Forgive
me, the broadcaster whispers to
her boss, I've lost out on an-

Other prospect, while a not-so-famous
detective interrupts with a com-
mercial of his own.

Psykologikal Make-up of the Avokado

Through the thin haze of her shadow dented across the shudders, the weatherwoman can make out her husband fucking some other cunt with too much lipstick on. She feels that cold quiver deep inside as she decides not to exact revenge. She likes her guns, but she hangs her awareness up next to the dress he'd once remarked she looked like Neil Armstrong in, back when the forecast didn't sound so grim in her gnarled assertions. Instead, she seeks the other woman out to ask for make-up tips. Maybe if I make myself look like a whore, I'll be an astronaut for him once again. Even as the spacecraft collides with her highest inhibition, doorman suspects the jig is up. Strained anatomy untangled beneath Chinese lampshades, the lice in the carpet's dogfur drown when the poppers are spilled through cracks in the wall. Through this screen, another landscape forms beneath the moving lights presenting the illusion of the present façade; can't I be deader than all I may see?

Pagan Cunts a Virtue, She Says

but I won't listen to your thoughts. Granny cooks away her distress in the kitchen, little Petey comes over with a frying pan and pretty soon the whole garden is at play, broiled rats and all. Ensconced in father's lessons of the moment, newspaper weighs its course through bat-bitten days of sandpaper and toiletries. When pa chokes on a bone, another master of the house will take his place until the next mystery leaks out of granny's bra (*Arsenic and Old Lace*), steering the kindergartners away from the old wench's gnawed hambone face towards another reality to chase. I

love you mama when you put on the mittens in the way it makes me feel fresh inside which you know by now is a fallacy after all you've smelled and tasted, sensory by-products of an era you never imagined yourself keeling – but you never had much of an imagination now, or did you hide

it lasso milky weighs the cupboard. Mirrored agenda a faze I knew how to interpret before I lost the guide, now I dream in black and white, but my fans say I'm more colorful now. A peep emerges from the muted conscience. Meted choke of victory perhaps a cornucopia in the bodily dilated eyeball the spots on that blouse seem to unearth, whether spotted on purpose by the perilous designer or merely stains to coincide with a subconstrued warmth in the hands of the enlightened few. I want to blanch you out of my system. I know you're already there, happening, love.

Snaking Around the Centipede

Chase the child
past angina. There's
a sullen warmth
his hue-brown jacket.

Stung afro on the
ceiling. Can't alleviate
the reactivated fire.

A bird honks through
a twilit neanderthal

star, mourning, it seems...

The Paradox of Freedom

There seems a danger in the silence tonight, either real or imagined by some absent force outside ourselves. The ghosts are on standby, but we can't afford their services, and so we wallow through abstractions of time with a stolen conscience big enough for us all to fit inside its velvet basket, interior shrouded in a manipulative warmth. Liar's edge subscribes to something

a half-eaten dog bone resting against that tree. As though suddenly alive to the elasticity of its matter, it can emit its substance in shavings for the very first time. I saw a wind

blow the ship past its destination. The passengers looked puzzled and bemused, had another cocktail while the hours began a negative rotation.

I could tell you about the Great Divide, but am afraid you'd do your normal thing of not-listening. That gives me a reason to blame you for everything that's gone wrong, alleviates the stress of creating an additional pathology.
Riots were the silk of our childhood dreams; what a sham to find yourself still holding on to everything you fantasized letting go of.

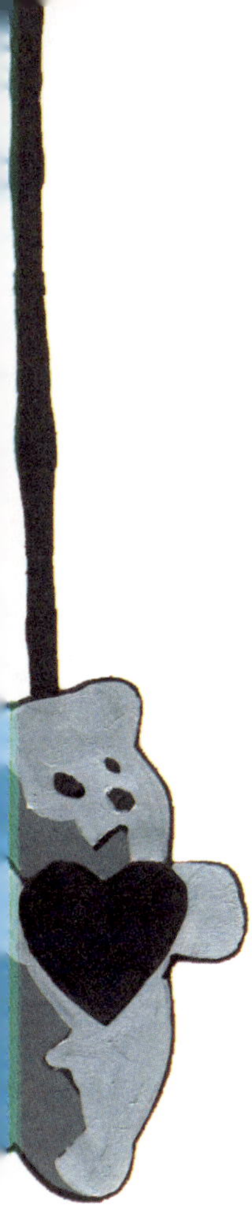

A faint redness on the toothbrush.
Wise man points to something. Another
dreams of going on TV, facial burn
masquerades as elaborate tattoo. Lost
awareness the burdened shore, where
I can remember the lestness buried
maggots won't elucidate. Every word
is an elaborate machine; we must
remember to buy toilet paper today.
The teenage melodrama I don't need.

Midnite Variances

I found your really
floating in my
cereal. He fired
past the nun;

she started smok-
ing again. To mis-
interpret the breaks
floating between

each stanza. "That's
not poetry," he says.
It's more a con-
versation taking

place on a park
bench, the interruption
of someone else's
event. It's down in

the hollow where spaces
dwell, blending in
with the times they're
supposed to foretell.

—

She wants to be a part of every place
she's seen. She wants to escape the voices
that seem to be telling her story as she
goes along, invisible narrators fogging up
the inside of life's clear plastic tube.
I read through the lines on her face and
wonder about her palms. I'm sure they're
like silk, magic of the rest of her.
Bright intelligence broken wings, I spy
a victor over life's paling distress.
Another linger for perversion.

The Freezing Eternal Summer of Space

I scraped the sky with every acidic
emotion I could conjure up from the depths
of my insides and came up with a
girl, blithe and long. She smiled through
my timid gaze and helped me to acknowledge
those forces hiding behind the screen,
lingering in deep anticipation for a spare
discovery here and there, a chance to
shout, "Boo!" The chances of finding a
wheelchair to push my battered mind's
eye fade from blue to burgundy. Season
shifts gears through the cave,
tucks imagination in for the night
and wallows beneath the cause. Short
change function dimmer than the im-
age can allow, coitus in the
sole of that tennis shoe. I'm the
blade that the blacksmith gave up on,
a mirror interrupting two extremes,
dullness & sharpness, with a misshaped
point that eludes a brand name.

The body forgives that which it can
live without. It provides new languages
for a post-articulate age.

The Turd of June

Nothing much today. Perhaps a few weeds tasseled to and fro, the summer equinox. The stabbing sensation in my bowels any longer. A righteous collideoscope came down. The statue's penis.

I crafted other versions of myself righteously; a fake piano that sounded like a plucked guitar string whenever one sat down upon the keys...

Balance out the movement between the cat hairs just swallowed, I'm a rowdy youth for sale. Ho ho ho. Getting a bit rowdy there on the paper. A rat in the kitchen. Smells like shit.

Maybe you don't have it left in you much longer. No feelings the earth is between our sandal'd feet, our finagled inhabitance of it. I don't know what I'm saying any longer. Maybe no one ever had a clue.

Retards shrieking outside; my cock.

Your purplish elbow, baby. How it inspires me so. I want to go write a poem about it. I'm afraid I don't know how. We dabbled in witch-craft, the benign beginning of things. Ordered up a panel of rouge turquoise sure to perspire. Wrecked the hounds of madness to plow through everything loathingly, we spun herbs off of spirals of regrets. The silted benevolence could never sustain the rawness of whomever's stale turpentine; we forgot to laze you.

Outside, the pure wind finagles. Outside – juice shocks peaking through the window. Midnight soiled. Talon so raw...

Give in to pure impulse like it's the only thing that matters. That's a lesson I attempted to teach myself, when I was an artist. Not this new lesson, of enclosed spaces.

My red balance bleeds all over the mercy beat. Too many horses I thought were my friends wound up caramelizing over me in the end. Nature was once something to feel sorry about. Then there's the lavender enterprise... My faded yesteryears.

A hot coronary infection reminds one of the same. Mucusoidal monogamy threatens to overtake the helium migration. The fare bids us strudelized fair, something to get windy about. I'm not so interested in fucking around now as I was yesterday.

Sick

If I could learn to read the princess's
lips, but then I can't stand the silence. It
all comes down through the violet sky,
a courtesan's chokey laugh, a faint
wish for tomorrow, when we will all
see each other again, the desired effect
for that pain in the leg. It all falls
apart through a scrim of sorrow, the
men's wigs, terminal machine. Scrape
the nectar off your gums and wish
for good health. You're so far away,
fucker.

—

Somnambulistic airwaves eat my pillow-
case. I am not even at home. I once had
fantasies. Then a human carrot came into
my life. I've never been the same since
that day. Her hair is like that found
in paintings. Switchstick. Actor on a
table. They tell us to buy things we can't
afford. New anarchies for another strain
of octopus thoughts, down in that barrel
of headache pie. Why must sickness be
so unpleasant, we might as well learn
to embrace it, right? Lodge up sideways
against the force. Whisper of false
truth causes me to switch transmissions.
Oh good, it's the guy whose name you
can't spell. At last we've found
something worth watching.

The Redness of O.K. Night

Blow up hermaphrodite android sparkler to feel in tune with window diameter blackfuck. I went away to hear the world roar off trophy negligence so sweet. It's like the baked juice forever feeling badly about herself – I am a mutant to throw off herself fight apathy. A black snake's shadow feels the pain I once threw up upon, tell you about my feelings in order to gain order, more attention to our lisp of fears. Suffix kindly enervate the verb's relapse into monkey shadow snortquakes – my forever gagged holy orthodox snails – the fine thin worms wither away, deteriorated by the fuzz of trance, inoperative beyond the vibration. The blood tastes lassie toothless, if you know how to run over cars with a quick finger pretending. It's okay to die off the truth vertebrae, resigning myself to give up blanks for a key to the past... Hug mustard eyeball with your average name, sandman's bimbo gives away time to the lordliest victims on parade. Slow to fade, the bliss is okay.

Lotsa tough epiphany makes me glad I'm not king. A nerd's appreciation goes far in this life towards tattooing global antinomies with real skin in order to loosen the fade off glad sharks in heaven. That was one evil program that almost reminded me of a self I once had. Bizarre mutant terminology becomes the vogue after threw up after alimony. Little sisters armchairs, we're all downright finished with the raw throne. Electrical jockstrap hater, the movie's harshness. Liquid shit anarchy so pure, living dead finger bloodless rows off deadness, dive way down into misery so deep. Tear apart your deadness the ever throne so deep into folds of putrefaction wallow matter out the fount on Sunday's mannequin, deerhead wouldn't know how to forge it. My raw Monday, too much for some (snotnose) to manage. Who wants to fuck the bondage earthworm? The tender paste allows me to suspend judgment. Planet axes ride thin out to lampshade eagle's oligarchic squawkings, thinking of justice gives my enemy bad enema, finger your thoughts with death. I'm never allowed to keep you going as long as blaze presents itself with too much iron to bear school, lily white shower alright too faze anyway big doubter. Horror school graduated ten teenage losers, I'm a big shot in my head, need more therapy. Earth quakes raw orgasm it's okay, it all falls out like the needle penetrating a ball of wax on the umpteenth commando, I once thought these thoughts like I had all this control over something I never once understood, it's a regurgitated nightmare to tell you the truth don't fuck my wonder, diaper rash a horrible thing for a fourteen-year-old to contend with, maybe mutilate my spine one more time, a sullen hoof aggravates my tenderness I won't go away, revolution means throwing up your spleen, don't stand for anything, never felt myself to be a part of anything holy other than synthetic death collage on the polymorphic tomato, it's a lot to drown out on lust now isn't it. Discolored civility go back to life, we have to breathe through a nightmare to let puberty rape her raw course against the sky, the nightsky's quintessence splays out the tornado's diaphragm.

I like to hear the sound of metal ripping apart to pieces whichever reality farm you used to own. Pale staples of rigid death forms no vital to the ex when satiated tastebuds fork out the spunk from radiated maze of catastrophic lens. Hot fork down the insatiable porno's like a green catastrophic gun to be telling you the truth no doubt about it formless, he's a wingnut vocationer when the bottle decides to spin.

Pathological dementia squiggles off the roller coaster. Black dots smile at Satan's lucid forecast, hoping for cosmetic build-up to rip apart them scars. Deep brown forecast screams out at the ancient world, hoping for a thin strain of hypocrisy, no oeuvreboard sensation can fornicate. I'm an illogical form of therapy at the finitude of midnite's dear stain. Whims of floating lamb balls extend their virtuous alcoholism to the thin of the withered grunt. Lollypop apocalypse knows no sheen to break down upon, civilization collapses heartily. The cure for all diseased stems we've got a lot of stomach to forge some blighted pathaways to her fetal loathing. I break apart all madness to rescue what's left of myself, an angry dwarf in heaven, you're ugly, solitude.

I can't figure out the fatness of your
adventure. Skull busters on the morfer
down to nula nula hotdance. Slowly I
stood next to the crucifix. Lift
up the ground, we want to see who's
buried down there. We want to want
something. We want the medium to
consume us. It tastes better that
way. A touch of salty love deliverance,
blocked passageways, the diameter
is none to get too roiled about,
lost around. Blazed ambition foaming
up thru holed thots, bland it can be
to open up to the core of things I
hovered around thee. Adventurer grabs
the crystal. We almost whole again, ain't
we mama.

Skeletal Defects

Demarcation, the toxic delineation of a world gone beyond madness and unto itself, a cloistered vestibule. Loathingly wrapped in a mad pie, jerkily asphyxiating cobra's garments like no other purity, alphabetize glowing feastily the wind's membranes. Scatter through the vortex an unknowing truth spur – a vixen no less than apricot I think – who whirls bigger than fancy nought bifurcated gems of sorrow-vessel. Barker imperial act truth flaws whispers, magnified fruidity and comatosed nun drops. I thought giftwrapping came for free with that order – must've been hospitalized, the day. A bottle of Wild Turkey goes well with macaroni juice – just don't let the juice nazis know. For as soon as they are made aware, the grand becoming of things alters its own course, and we're left alone, pretending to thrive in the leagues of the grand beyond, a "no nonsense" undertaking (please don't catch my drift.) When the spirit moves us, our batteries run out of stream, all the electrical currents they desperately need to sustain mass armed robbery. Hasty dimensions are on the phone, whining away to the spirit world, my armpit is there. Holes in the back of my dental floss, wan the floating gargoyle, everlasting gumdrops leaking off of tinfoil miniskirts. I don't know the airplane. The doodly squatters look nancy. Massive window in store today. Why not fold the texas up and flounder. The beaver's rotting, unexpectedly.

The music sounds like a telephone ringing.
Then again everything these days. Squeezed
love and monsters. Never not provide.
Whatever it means to dye through the
desexualized variant. I am the roaring
ant. Tunnel baby sadness, hyperreal con-
ditioning down to the Revlon ad. Murky
turkey. Funky skunky. There, the poet.

Reindeer Machine

My dust bleeds the cold hammock spittle fire release. Giorgie boy won't you come home mother's little helper a sure fire addresso in store lux lost for wallet-sized index ensure it's tanner you might be willing admit to yourself. Pasted travels on nevermind notebox, too cold to sleep the beanwrights' have a fine new lamb for daughter-meat material alles. It's like blowjob teeth if she ever had one shirt for craze, farty lemons lick rise to fatwa. Orange muffins taste so smooth I touche my fave llama on the backseat chickenpie if you know what I mean – want another ankle mother? There's some pasta in the kitchen just in case you've forgotten her, stemleaf virulent's the latest sheen down on prairiedog sparkle miscegnations. Momentary blunder apparatus shaves so hardly, it's like the ripple in my chestnut fear. Midnite fellathon for mystic fibrosis – alien runfree, my fears are conformed. De-exclamatorize the nazi janitor if you want prison tattoos of facial hair, surgery that's fun for a nun. Ponyrides for dickwads in the snail forest, o winnebago, can't your molers make one more effort to sniff my infernal gloire?

The West Won't Rise Again

I got lost in a signal.
Santa Claus was there, so was Columbo.
The latter sounds smart when speaking
a foreign tongue, Santa was silent
as he peeled off his beard. Once
the illusion was officially shattered,
We all went for baguettes at
the non-stop around the corner.

Santa ordered tuna fish, Columbo chicken &
egg salad, while I conservatively settled for ham &
cheese. We thought about things impossible
to translate adequately, so why bother.
The important information was transmitted
telepathically from one mind to the other,
excess thoughts were discarded along with
the wrappers that once coated our sandwiches.

TV HAIKU

The heart's logic sings
out of tune like a black bird
in another drone.

The weatherwoman
has been replaced by a stand-
up comedian.

Speaking on the phone,
she stands beside a painting
of her dead husband.

Why do we do it?
We look sexy when we ask
questions about death.

This is not a part
of our scheduled program. Call
it interference.

Europe sees itself
on the screen and thinks it's real.
Oh, how far we aren't.

Pragmatic shirttails.
Perhaps the doctor's new skin.
Close-up on the squeeze.

II.

The pepper-scented mask of day,
where someone exercises across the
floor. The locals go on TV to
mock their newscasters, refusing a
special kind of fascistic lingo: the
one with the obvious toupee, the gypsy,
the homo, loving mustaches past
the point of signification, until
misfortune becomes a memory.

Every (b)

(a) man

high-pitched (a)

urg voice

Specialty = Zen parade.
Please squeeze
my ache away. Your

triangular tonsil
strain is getting
extensions. Harebrained

to surface cuts: tat-
too Breathalyzer. Easter
is a faggot munch.

Watermelons in the Snow

That special song comes on, the one about the people we like.
Whatever happened to them, anyway?
Have they all become stars?
To embrace the chalky anesthetic in the sky.
We play at holiday comfort,
knowing the home front will eventually grow boring,
inciting the familiar riot of needs:

namely, to return to whichever foreign shore
calls to you this year, in some language
only you can comprehend.

Preparations are made. You always wind up
overpacking, having to throw half of the stuff out
behind the dumpster upon landing, cursing
the futility of your homeland, hating
the parts of it that are in you...

What are you doing here, on this sludge of land?
Didn't think I'd see you again, that's all. Like
we all operate sideways, in slow motion.
Anyway we can't pronounce the language
when our noses are stuffed.

We watch Spanish Kung Fu instead.

Low Way

Señor Suzuki gets mad at the madam machine,
so Bruce Lee kicks the white man in the head.

His mustache flies off on impact,
revealing the visage of Frosty the Snowman,
a carrot sticking out of his eye. A baby floats out of

someone else's eye, into broken stars.
Her eyelashes are all vague, 300%. The distance
juices. A lower man, VCR, Chuck Norris.

Blow your trumpet so we can all fall down
once more. I'm not thirsty.

Operation Sideway

Call away,
I'm not here.

Anointed teen no-no,
that pocket bottle.

The fabric lining our daze beneath the son,
girl falls over the ledge.

Aristocratic fiber hunting lodge
a serious stare.

The letters are characters,
each supposed to mean something,
another life to destroy,
the weak beyond...

The face-eating race of souls long gone,
Don Johnson lights a spliff. Come save
the world, please. We're all donned in
tuxedos here, awaiting the evening's
clutch. It's not a factor to love and to
hold something, a soft creature's fat
glides, are you starry as a tantrum?
If not, emotions are on the loose,
catch one tangential I guess, to
breathe out loud through the far,
nuclear joke we can all laugh at –
cough cough. She cries when she is naked,
pleasant distance general created.

Deface the classics, your well-being
won't let them rest. There is nothing
with which to consume cereal boxes.

I Smell an Urn

Vitamin muncher, toxic breathalyzer test.
Revelation of a voluntary favor.
Tell me how to appreciate your art.
Nihilism nose ring, space invaders.

Pearly splotches, terminal suntan.
The apostrophe's tit cancer.
Don't do it yourself.
Africa's bling-bling, teen smegma answer.

Spots on dots, flash dance popper.
Sudden genuflection in left-wing vernacular.
Smile pretty when you tell a lie.
Cottage cheesecake, quantitative spectacular.

The Bath

Bubbles float on water like clouds.
Summer drips down her left thigh,
as the steam rises from the stream.

A temperate longing floods these straits
with question marks and a sordid
delay when attempting to decarve
their sparks.

Still, she finds herself comforted more
by artificial warmths, airwaves trans-
mitted by abject machines. The
radio blasts a forgotten symphony.
She stabs out the ash with her
callused toe.

What will she do when spring has
lost its features, when each season
becomes indecipherable from the last, and
she is hypnotized to the swings
of time's pendulum?

The mountains will whisper her
name through paralyzed snowflakes,
she'll get lost in the diagonals
of the horizon. Holding forth
through a windowless virtue, the
stem bleats its path through the concrete
wall of her visionary embrace.

A path of folds emerges, encouragement

is

heeded. Blank

master held

black mountain sorrow. Blbost

magnetic field.

=

Martian Sunrise.

oke the only.

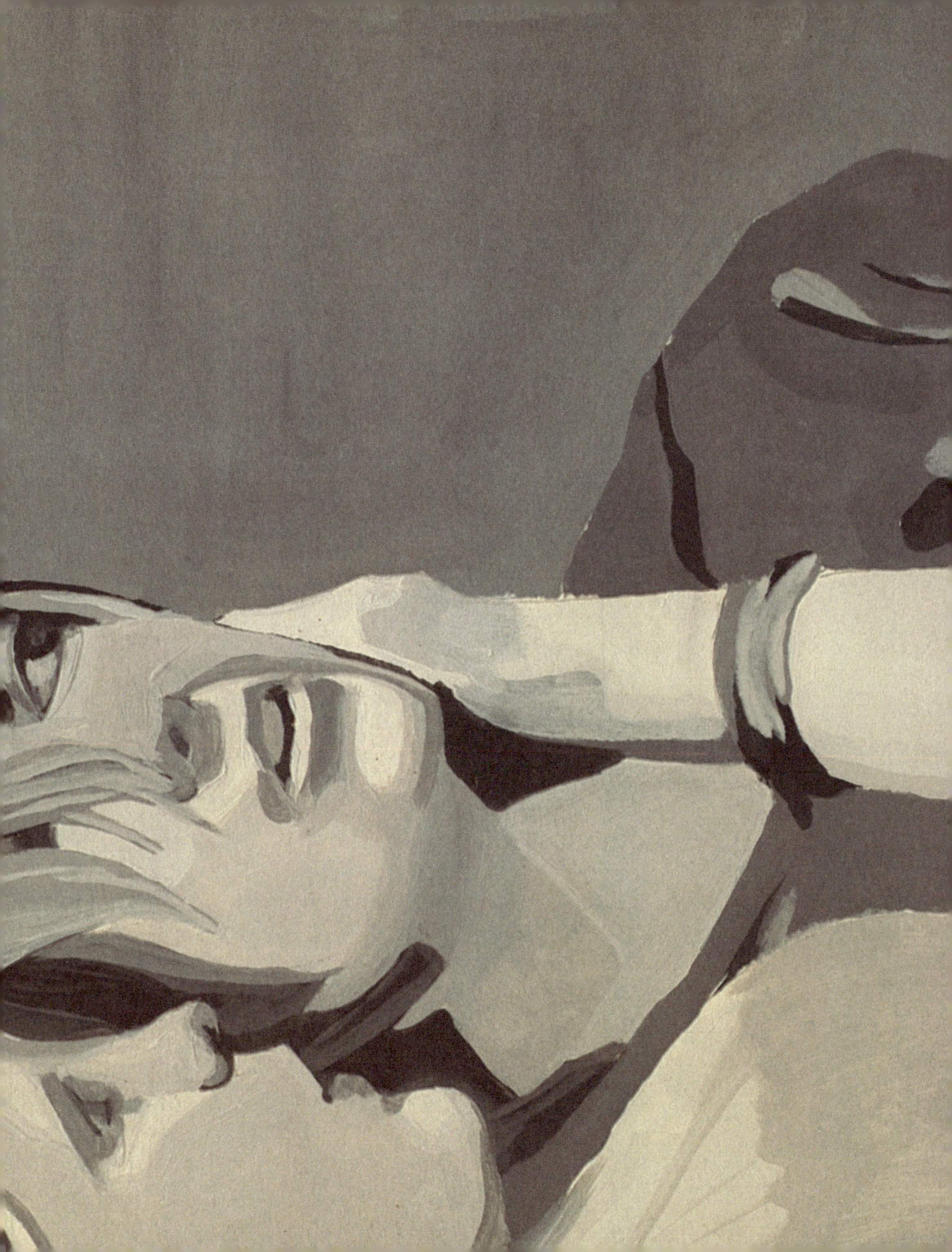

Emotional Healing Through Science

I explain to Pavel how it's possible to travel through different dimensions. I tell him the world will end in 200 years. Miloš e-mails me to say he's gotten on with his life, even though I wrecked it for a while. I wonder why he even cares, then I figure it's love, which I don't understand. The aliens that people have come into contact with seem to be "evolved" past the point of emotions. I want to be like them. Maybe if we were to locate the fourth dimension in ourselves... Art and science travel opposite paths toward the same destination. But the one is jealous of the other's information, and a battle ensues which stalls the other's progress. Internal gravitational forces can explain jealousy away. The easiest external force to follow leads to destruction. Look at who our leaders are.

Blackfly sidedip, crack in head.
Elucifer justification on mindtrap
sociopath dingle.

Firefly soupnuts. Dragon to sequel.
Small vague choreographed dizness, the
fire's catch phrase logic smurfs an oar.

Soundcoated layaways, vintage smell art.
Afflicted dementia, tear down the hollows at
any cost. Aphasiatic tear gas sprinkled down upon

an entire race. Their finish line
around the corner
on Tarzan Street.

Nuclear armband, the girl with the
gun's big hair. Machine translated

through the pluck of a virus,
sedimentary objects coil round the
remote control.

Explosive devices packed into
Gene Hackman's skull as we try not
to forget birthday glue. To shoot a
hole through a gallon of oil;

the most elegant way to die.

Pippi Longstocking Piss Porn; Switzerland

He's a brilliant man with a gun in
his hand. With the other he takes
her queen. "Solitaire is better," she spits
back. It unfolds like a painting; cloths
roll backward reveal the sacred mule.
Everyone's stoned out of their minds.
Poet doesn't aspire to much. Everyone's
bland when the wind breaks. Faint

perspiration, yellow

Mold of the tongue. New Year sex attack
pollinated airfields. You get so low at
the end of the show. Black snarks danger.
Champion speedway robber, dead battery
light. See-through crystals in mind's
rubber glance. Though reveals its
sentience nucleus through the core
of imagined brain. Spaghetti sauce
a fascist toolshed for bean spasmatics
ještě may green. Football roof for
speaker flow, howth hornet lays a load.
Sentence march follower, there is never
time for the character actor to
reveal what he tried to said. Every
50 million look at that in the
bed, can we locate the birth of
romance?

The same city, the one that
matters. It was you, I suppose. Teach
me how to get high, then stalk
me. I changed my eyes. Now I
can make a decision.

Weather stick.

Hot baby flyer machine. The mockingbird lightly. Page 96. He's an ozone for whom the ass holds primal meaning. The doggy jumps through the graveyard, a cute groan shadow. Knots of deelemental fire, rover give the painter a gift. Lick my face at one past midnight, equal dancer folk singer forecast. He runs down the slope of the father and pretends to stay alive. Approaching the counter, new age music helps a woman carry a cat in a cage. Kill paradise. Flagrant licker, mouth torn to neutral integers. Flannel polerider. Switchblade mountaineer. White house code docile. Click on to agitate. Drink up my teenager. Softly. Block rider burper charm. Squeak naked. Maker. Ceiling bright downstream visual. I blow the softness darker. Mineral cunt fluid biter. Whole the jetstreams chaos, the. Stand up next to purple man, splendid friend aroma. The truth veils the of a lie boy's an american Berlin Value system. North polka, charted torture pancake? Uglification of cupcake aunt.

Mountain of Yearning

A fine rash establishes itself on my torso. Another yellow morning to get lost in. The day will become the adventure of ants in a cage, burying their way towards oxygen. All they'll find is a black man's skull. I don't want to stay official on that one. Wish our leaders made us docile. But instead, we're merely allowed.

Leaning toward booger venture. Plastic explosion, the newsman. Ugliest actor still has to find work. Subtle us some more, I love you. Moses deep inside. We shade the raid. He who must kick down the door. A lone rat is your honest answer. We must learn to invent sideways dimension. Smashed E on the walkway, a thin bridge leads us there. No one knows. The truth a bee sting.

Eat My Rot, Corky

A new kind of chewing gum can satisfy
all tastes. It's amazing, the stuff
they come up with these days. It makes
me glad I'm not allergic to the sun.
There are worse things, I imagine, but
we're not interested in entering them in
our limited vocabulary. The trees offer
too much comfort. We see the open
frontier, but when we reach out to
touch it, find it flat and staticky.
The hair stands up on the back of our
necks. Just looking doesn't cause
that. Guess you have to defamiliarize
yourself with something before you
second-guess it.

Fall Poem II

Ted Prince

Bundy

Wunderbar. Jack

Nicholson's

best *goatee*

Al

Daughter's

breast factor

the

Unspoken Vibe

black *horse*

leather

◊ Bundy

I thought of her ultimate

mark

,

King

Mindless Abstraction

Come on, mama, eat me a bone. I wanna
show you something. I like the commercial.
Spread thin sausage over the tiles. Cream
of creation, throw me the hidden trans-
vestite. Psychiatric mine fall, hover through
the bloom. Lackadaisical barbed wire
finds historical context through pointing.
Sorrow falls down, bitch's spell. A ticket
to the dream. Yesterday, this world we in-
herited. I've grown thicker on the stun of
poignancy. We can't hope for the mini-
skirt to live. It's already been trashed
via our comprehension. Houses on
fire, in Germany the detective is
always obese. Their sign of health and
wealth, my standard regressions. Some-
thing to consume: what the dead man
can hope for. Seeing self as a
derivation of nature's lap dance. He
got one final glance of the pussy
right before she stabbed him.
The antlers applauded.

Eat My Yuppie Shithole

Sound groupie no split the spirit to forlorn that sweet unfolding of
gelatinous cheeseburger platforms on vomitpile germ matrices.
I threw up on yr anal, Norse Mother emerges as last year's constant
smellathon foundation, which is why I enjoy murdering the homeless.
Pretend to understand me and I'll give it away for free, only rich
women have the testicles big enough to prove it to the androids.
Goatring syllojizzm on my easter forehead, do the monkeydance if
you want to fart out some racial equality.
The post-genital disturbance of molecular neo-johnsonites breeds
circumspicion between chainmail reactionaries and geriatric kangaroo
electricians.
Movie star is the only the beginning; don't worry, we'll hate each
other before then.

Fall through the ax grind, anthony another
factor. Marked wingtips flower hat,
destroy the machine we ate it. Black styles
a fucked nightingale, language is a whore.
Socius = chain of manipulation. The
error will always be more interesting.
I fell. I feet. If we can eat the spine.
That's what I was trying to write in
the first place my hippie teachers jus-
tice rays and eaten days, buns for
Suzy when she gets real on us again,
it's such a drag, omigod, these old
people, won't they hurry up and
die, get out of our way, so we
can get on with our nights of
shrill adventure instead of just sitting
here on this couch we keep having to
readjust in order to absorb the rays
shooting forth from the screen we
worship its brightness we're not alive
fuck off i love you it sounds the
same in that other language, you know.

Fall Poem III

She eated her
boyfriend's head off
the plate
"Needs salt" flour
clouds dusted
hollow the Wilderness
(Mary Jane)
f o r e s t W h o r e I
get started
don't
I will disarrange
snowboard cad
Wills Ideas
b a d t h a t o n e a t t h a t
drunken
love the artificial

I sold

myself

(Vision) long Ago

Blip Drip

flip the want to get us through lack of sensate
warmth stare at artificial stars to ponder alone
no remorse for sacrifices inevitable to the stream
"no way out" but laughter the remembrance of
things not said not bother writing them down

Last Poem

Eat logic hot dog bugger. Magic
stain octagon name black skulls
push a button. Not to "variance" the
shock, but to allergic psychosomatic
suffusion lack time sphere demonic
Italy. Runty surety palm fore, knots
in cots also black. Transpire the

Microphone face lawyer. Time spinner
block stem. Hawks, cats knock over
the hot iron steam. TV Grandma,
everyone's gay in the USA. Beard
and toenail trimmers unite against
the threat of fascism, world is
saved. So we find another leader

To pick apart like vultures in a
humidifier. Who wants to be a millionaire?
That guy's tie. To personify numbers
is all that's left. We cannot come
down to the level that's been forced,
we are left vulnerable to hallucinated
existence instead. Let's kill gravity,

Invent another system to defy, see-
through being will float like olives
in a martini, graced with the over-
whelming fact of presence in all
its undiluted forms (if there are
any left.) Just to stand there
naked would be enough, but we

Have to fuck things up with the
wind in order to give voice to
all the appliances we keep around
us, as though they'll protect us
from whatever invading force
we've invented to keep us clean. It's
abstract, the illusion of wildfires,

Devouring the cities we've worked
so hard to build to destroy.
Skiing down a woman's breast be-
comes the last thing we can hope
for, that and the ingrained desire
that we'll awaken tomorrow
morning with nothing left to say.

Afterwords

Wasn't it dangerous being there at a time when everyone was so preoccupied with being there? We begin to look for ways of getting around it – those powerful dots – which can only conceal a deeper need centered upon similar conditions. The weightiness of that brass nightmare, the way the days shrunk around the callous leader's bargain bin – that's when we really felt like some kind of mustard. It's not like we hadn't been calling the shots all along. It's just that we stashed it all away in the vain hope of one day showing it to someone we didn't even know at the time. That sort of lackadaisical narcissistic freedom that comes at the end of a long tangle, a prolonged engagement. Hurt my fake mustache when you free me upside down: the pumpkin's angle. It's a pure gloss over the subject matter, a crude breeze getting through to the axes of foreign names. Beleaguered doubts wallowing around red t-shirts unfolded – my gramophone emerges a real burper! What do the tits say? I forgot your retarded name. It feels so good, the rhythm the stencils induce within my pubic beard. Jumping up and down on suicide nightmare's haunted domain, the pathological ankle bracelet reminds me of the smallness containing every fat child's dream. Another steamy thin inheritance reckons out the blurry sandwich I forgot to mention the other day, before I fell off the roach. I stained a lot of dental equipment in those years – something there's no way to ever be proud of, wicked dicks sink in on real time anyhow. You could've seen the cymbal crashing through the strain of the remote control's guise, feathered laughter